The Measure
of a Man

FACETS

The Measure of a Man

Martin Luther King Jr.

OTIRA
AND
FAMILY.

Fortress Press
Minneapolis

Library of Congress Cataloging-in-Publication Data

King, Martin Luther, Jr., 1929–1968.

The measure of a man.
1. Man (Christian theology) I. Title.
BT703.K5   1988   233   87–45898
ISBN 0–8006–0877–1

Printed in the United States of America   1-877

10 09 08 07   13 14 15 16 17 18

What Is Man?

The question "What is man?" is one of the most important questions confronting any generation. The whole political, social, and economic structure of a society is largely determined by its answer to this pressing question. Indeed, the conflict which we witness in the world today between totalitarianism and democracy is at bottom a conflict over the question "What is man?"

In our generation the asking of this question has risen to extensive proportions. But although there is widespread agreement in asking the question, there is fantastic disagreement in answering it. For instance, there are those who look upon man as little more than an animal. They would say that man is a cosmic accident, that his whole life can be explained by matter in motion. Then there are those who would lift man almost to the position of a god. They would probably agree with Shakespeare's Hamlet, "What a piece of work is man! How noble in faculty! How infinite in reason; in form and moving how express and admirable; in apprehension how like a God; in action how like an angel! The beauty of the world, the paragon of animals."

There are still others who would seek to be a little more realistic about man. They would avoid the extremes of a pessimistic naturalism and an optimistic humanism and seek to combine the truths of both. They see within man a strange dualism, something of a dichotomy. So they would cry out with Carlyle, "There are depths in man that go down to the lowest hell, and heights that reach the highest heaven, for are not both heaven and hell made out of him—everlasting miracle and mystery that he is?"

One day the psalmist looked up and noticed the vastness of the cosmic order. He noticed the infinite expanse of the solar system; he noticed the beautiful stars; he gazed at the moon with all its scintillating beauty, and he said in the midst of all of this, "What is man?" He comes forth with an answer: "Thou hast made him a little lower than the angels, and crowned him with glory and honor." Goodspeed, Moffatt, and the Revised Standard would say, "Thou hast made him a little less than divine, a little less than God, and crowned him with glory and honor." It is this realistic position that I would like to use as a basis of our thinking together and our meditation on the question "What is man?"

Now let us notice first that man is a biological being with a physical body. This is why the psalmist says, "Thou hast made him less than God." We don't think of God as a being with a body. God is a being of pure spirit, lifted above the categories of time and space; but man, being less than God, is in time. He is in nature, and he can never disown his kinship with animate nature.

The psalmist goes on to say that God made man that way. Since God made him that way there is nothing wrong with it. We read in the Book of Genesis that everything God makes is good; therefore there is nothing wrong with having a body. This is one of the things that distinguish the Christian doctrine of man from the Greek doctrine. The Greeks, under the impetus of Plato, felt that the body was evil, almost inherently depraved, and the soul could never reach its full maturity until it broke loose from the prison of the body. This is not Christian doctrine, for Christianity does not see the body as the principle of evil; it says the will is the principle of evil.

So the body in Christianity is sacred and significant. That means in any doctrine of man that we must be concerned with man's physical well-being. It may be true that man cannot live by bread alone, but the mere fact that Jesus added the "alone" means that man cannot live without bread. Religion must never overlook this, and any religion that professes to be concerned about the souls of men and is not concerned about the economic conditions that damn the soul, the social conditions that corrupt men, and the city governments that cripple them, is a dry, dead, do-nothing religion in need of new blood. For it overlooks the basic fact that man is a biological being with a physical body. This must stand as a principle in any doctrine of man.

But this isn't the only part, and we must never stop here if our doctrine of man is to be realistic and thoroughly Christian. Some people stop here. They are the naturalists or the materialists; they are the Marxists; and they would see man merely as an animal.

Some years ago a group of chemists who had a flair for statistics decided to work out the worth of man's body in terms of the market values of that day. They got together and did a lot of work, and finally they came to this conclusion: The average man has enough fat in him to make about seven bars of soap, enough iron to make a medium-sized nail, enough sugar to fill a shaker, enough lime to whitewash a chicken coop, enough phosphorus for about 2,220 match tips, and enough magnesium for a dose of magnesia. When all of this was added up in terms of the market values of that day it came to about ninety-eight cents. Now, I guess, since the standards of living are a little higher today, you could get about a dollar ninety-eight for the average man.

This is interesting. Think about it. Man's bodily stuff is worth only ninety-eight cents. But can we explain the whole of man in terms of ninety-eight cents? Can we explain the artistic genius of a Michelangelo in terms of ninety-eight cents? Can we explain the poetic genius of a Shakespeare in terms of ninety-eight cents? Can we explain the spiritual genius of Jesus of Nazareth in terms of ninety-eight cents? Can we explain the mystery of the human soul in terms of ninety-eight cents? Oh, no. There is something within man that cannot be explained in terms of dollars and cents. There is something within man that cannot be reduced to chemical and biological terms, for man is more than a tiny vagary of whirling electrons. He is more than a wisp of smoke from a limitless smoldering. Man is a child of God.

This brings us to another basic point in the doctrine of man—that man is a being of spirit. This is what the psalmist means when he says, "Thou hast crowned him with glory and honor." Man has rational capacity; man has a mind; man can reason. This distinguishes him from the lower animals. And so, somehow, man is in nature, and yet he is above nature; he is in time, and yet he is above time; he is in space, and yet he is above space. This means that he can do things that lower animals could never do. He can think a poem and write it; he can think a symphony and compose it; he can think up a great civilization and create it.

Man is God's marvelous creation, crowned with glory and honor, and because of this you can't quite hem him in. You can put him in Bedford's prison, but somehow his mind will break out through the bars to scratch a *Pilgrim's Progress* across the pages of history. You can bring him down in his wretched old age, with his body broken down and his vision all but gone, and yet in the form of a Handel, he will look up and imagine that he hears the very angels singing, and he will come back and scratch across the pages of history a "Hallelujah Chorus."

This is man. He is God's marvelous creation. Through his mind he can leap oceans, break through walls, and transcend the categories of time and space. The stars may be marvelous, but not so marvelous as the mind of man that comprehended them.

This is what the biblical writers mean when they say that man is made in the image of God. Man has rational capacity; he has the unique ability to have fellowship with God. Man is a being of spirit.

There is another principle that must go in any doctrine of man that is realistic. It is the recognition that man is a sinner. Man is a free being made in the image of God. He is different from lower animals. He is not guided merely by instinct. He has the ability to choose between alternatives, so he can choose the good or the evil, the high or the low.

As we look at man, we must admit that he has misused his freedom. Some of the image of God is gone. Therefore, man is a sinner in need of God's divine grace. So often we try to deny this fact. We hate to face it. There are times even in our theological thinking when we have become all too sentimental about man.

We have explained his shortcomings in terms of errors or lags of nature. We have sometimes felt that progress was inevitable, and that man was gradually evolving into a higher state of perfection. But if we are honest and realistic, we must admit that it isn't like that, for man is a sinner. We take the new depth psychology, and misuse it to explain our bad deeds. We find ourselves saying that they are due to phobias, to inner conflicts. Or, in Freudian terms, we say that man's misdeeds are due to a conflict between the id and the superego.

But when we look at ourselves hard enough we come to see that the conflict is between God and man. There is something within all of us that causes us to see the truth in Plato's statement that the personality is like a charioteer with two headstrong horses, each wanting to go in different directions. There is something within all of us that causes us to cry out with Augustine, "Lord, make me pure, but not yet." There is something within all of us that causes us to affirm with the apostle Paul, "The good that I would, I do not; and the evil that I would not, I do." And so in a real sense the "isness" of our present nature is out of harmony with the eternal "oughtness" that forever confronts us. We know how to love, and yet we hate. We take the precious lives that God has given us and throw them away in riotous living. We are unfaithful to those to whom we should be faithful. We are disloyal to those ideals to which we should be loyal. "All we like sheep have gone astray."

I don't know about you, but when I look at myself hard enough I don't feel like crying with the Pharisee, "Lord, I thank thee that I am not like other men," but I find myself crying out, "Lord, be merciful unto me, a sinner." We are sinners in need of God's divine grace. When we come to our collective lives, our sin is even greater. One theologian could write a book entitled *Moral Man and Immoral Society.* In our collective lives our sin rises to even greater heights. See how we treat each other. Races trample over races; nations trample over nations. We go to war and destroy the values and the lives that God has given us. We leave the battlefields of the world painted with blood, and we end up with wars that burden us with national debts higher than mountains of gold, filling our nations with orphans and widows, sending thousands of men home psychologically deranged and physically handicapped.

This is the tragic plight of man. As we look at all of that, we know that man isn't made for that. We know that man is made for the stars, created for the everlasting, born for eternity. We know that man is crowned with glory and honor, and so long as he lives on the low level he will be frustrated, disillusioned, and bewildered.

Jesus told a parable one day, the parable of the prodigal son. He talked about a boy who left home and went away into a far country, where he wasted his substance and even his character. Then a famine broke out, and this boy ended up in a hogpen.

There are many insights to be gained from this parable. One, I think, is this: that man is not made for the far country of evil. Whenever he moves away from his Father's house he finds himself facing a famine, and he finds himself frustrated and disillusioned. But the parable does not end there. That's the beauty of it. We read that one day the boy came to himself and decided to rise up and go back home. We watch him as he travels up the dusty road that he had once come down. He had a little speech that he had made up: "I am not worthy of being called thy son." But he did not get a chance to make that speech, because a loving father saw him from afar and ran out to the boy with outstretched arms, saying, "I am happy to have you back home. Come home, I still love you."

This is the glory of our religion: that when man decides to rise up from his mistakes, from his sin, from his evil, there is a loving God saying, "Come home, I still love you."

Oh, I can hear a voice crying out today,

saying to Western civilization: "You strayed away to the far country of colonialism and imperialism. You have trampled over one billion six hundred million of your colored brothers in Africa and Asia. But, O Western Civilization, if you will come to yourself, rise up, and come back home, I will take you in."

It seems that I can hear a voice saying to America: "You started out right. You wrote in your Declaration of Independence that 'all men are created equal and endowed by their Creator with certain inalienable rights. Among these are life, liberty, and the pursuit of happiness.' But, America, you strayed away from that sublime principle. You left the house of your great heritage and strayed away into a far country of segregation and discrimination. You have trampled over sixteen million of your brothers. You have deprived them of the basic goods of life. You have taken from them their self-respect and their sense of dignity. You have treated them as if they were things rather than persons. Because of this a famine has broken out in your land. In the midst of all your material wealth, you are spiritually and morally poverty-stricken, unable to speak to the conscience of this world. America, in this famine situation, if you will come to yourself and rise up and decide to come back home, I will take you in, for you are made for something high and something noble and something good."

To every man there openeth
A Way, and Ways, and a Way,
And the High Soul climbs the High Way,
And the Low Soul gropes the Low,
And in between, on the misty flats,
The rest drift to and fro.
But to every man there openeth
A High Way, and a Low,
And every man decideth
The Way his soul shall go.

—John Oxenham

O God, our gracious heavenly Father, we thank thee for the inspiration of Jesus the Christ, who came to this world to show us the way. And grant that we will see in that life the fact that we are made for that which is high and noble and good. Help us to live in line with that high calling, that great destiny. In the name of Jesus we pray. Amen.

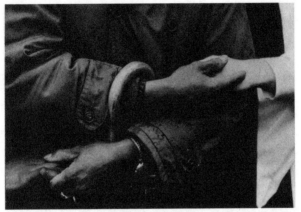

Schulke Archives

© 1986 Flip Schulke

The Dimensions of a
Complete Life

Many, many centuries ago, out on a lonely, obscure island called Patmos, a man by the name of John caught a vision of the new Jerusalem descending out of heaven from God. One of the greatest glories of this new city of God that John saw was its completeness. It was not partial and one-sided, but it was complete in all three of its dimensions. And so, in describing the city in the twenty-first chapter of the book of Revelation, John says this: "The length and the breadth and the height of it are equal." In other words, this new city of God, this city of ideal humanity, is not an unbalanced entity but it is complete on all sides.

Now John is saying something quite significant here. For so many of us the book of Revelation is a very difficult book, puzzling to decode. We look upon it as something of a great enigma wrapped in mystery. And certainly if we accept the book of Revelation as a record of actual historical occurrences it is a difficult book, shrouded with impenetrable mysteries. But if we will look beneath the peculiar jargon of its author and the prevailing apocalyptic symbolism, we will find in this book many eternal truths which continue to challenge us. One such truth is that of this text. What John is really saying is this: that life as it should be and life at its best is the life that is complete on all sides.

There are three dimensions of any complete life to which we can fitly give the words of this text: length, breadth, and height. The length of life as we shall think of it here is not its duration or its longevity, but it is the push of a life forward to achieve its personal ends and ambitions. It is the inward concern for one's own welfare. The breadth of life is the outward concern for the welfare of others. The height of life is the upward reach for God.

These are the three dimensions of life, and without the three being correlated, working harmoniously together, life is incomplete. Life is something of a great triangle. At one angle stands the individual person, at the other angle stand other persons, and at the top stands the Supreme, Infinite Person, God. These three must meet in every individual life if that life is to be complete.

Now let us notice first the length of life. I have said that this is the dimension of life in which the individual is concerned with developing his inner powers. It is that dimension of life in which the individual pursues personal ends and ambitions. This is perhaps the selfish dimension of life, and there is such a thing as moral and rational self-interest. If one is not concerned about himself he cannot be totally concerned about other selves.

Some years ago a learned rabbi, the late Joshua Liebman, wrote a book entitled *Peace of Mind*. He has a chapter in the book entitled "Love Thyself Properly." In this chapter he says in substance that it is impossible to love other selves adequately unless you love your own self properly. Many people have been plunged into the abyss of emotional fatalism because they did not love themselves properly. So every individual has a responsibility to be concerned about himself enough to discover what he is made for. After he discovers his calling he should set out to do it with all of the strength and power in his being. He should do it as if God Almighty called him at this particular moment in history to do it. He should seek to do his job so well that the living, the dead, or the unborn could not do it better. No matter how small one thinks his life's work is in terms of the norms of the world and the so-called big jobs, he must realize that it has cosmic significance if he is serving humanity and doing the will of God.

To carry this to one extreme, if it falls your lot to be a street sweeper, sweep streets as Raphael painted pictures, sweep streets as Michelangelo carved marble, sweep streets as Beethoven composed music, sweep streets as Shakespeare wrote poetry. Sweep streets so well that all the hosts of heaven and earth will have to pause and say, "Here lived a great street sweeper who swept his job well." In the words of Douglas Mallock:

> If you can't be a highway, just be a trail;
> If you can't be the sun, be a star;
> For it isn't by size that you win
>   or you fail—
> Be the best of whatever you are.

When you do this, you have mastered the first dimension of life—the length of life.

But don't stop here; it is dangerous to stop here. There are some people who never get beyond this first dimension. They are brilliant people; often they do an excellent job in developing their inner powers; but they live as if nobody else lived in the world but themselves. There is nothing more tragic than to find an individual bogged down in the length of life, devoid of the breadth.

The breadth of life is that dimension of life in which we are concerned about others. An individual has not started living until he can rise above the narrow confines of his individualistic concerns to the broader concerns of all humanity.

You remember one day a man came to Jesus and he raised some significant questions. Finally he got around to the question "Who is my neighbor?" This could easily have been a very abstract question left in midair. But Jesus immediately pulled that question out of midair and placed it on a dangerous curve between Jerusalem and Jericho. He talked about a certain man who fell among thieves. Three men passed; two of them on the other side. And finally another man came and helped the injured man on the ground. He is known to us as the good Samaritan. Jesus says in substance that this is a great man. He was great because he could project the "I" into the "thou."

So often we say that the priest and the Levite were in a big hurry to get to some ecclesiastical meeting and so they did not have time. They were concerned about that. I would rather think of it another way. I can well imagine that they were quite afraid. You see, the Jericho road is a dangerous road, and the same thing that happened to the man who was robbed and beaten could have happened to them. So I imagine the first question that the priest and the Levite asked was this: "If I stop to help this man, what will happen to me?" Then the good Samaritan came by, and by the very nature of his concern reversed the question: "If I do not stop to help this man, what will happen to him?" And so this man was great because he had the mental equipment for a dangerous altruism. He was great because he could surround the length of his life with the breadth of life. He was great not only because he had ascended to certain heights of economic security, but because he could condescend to the depths of human need.

All this has a great deal of bearing in our situation in the world today. So often racial groups are concerned about the length of life, their economic privileged position, their social status. So often nations of the world are concerned about the length of life, perpetuating their nationalistic concerns, and their economic ends. May it not be that the problem in the world today is that individuals as well as nations have been overly concerned with the length of life, devoid of the breadth? But there is still something to remind us that we are interdependent, that we are all involved in a single process, that we are all somehow caught in an inescapable network of mutuality. Therefore whatever affects one directly affects all indirectly.

As long as there is poverty in the world I can never be rich, even if I have a million dollars. As long as diseases are rampant and millions of people in this world cannot expect to live more than twenty-eight or thirty years, I can never be totally healthy even if I just got a good checkup at Mayo Clinic. I can never be what I ought to be until you are what you ought to be. This is the way our world is made. No individual or nation can stand out boasting of being independent. We are interdependent. So John Donne placed it in graphic terms when he affirmed, "No man is an island entire of itself. Every man is a piece of the continent, a part of the main." Then he goes on to say, "Any man's death diminishes me because I am involved in mankind, and therefore never send to know for whom the bell tolls; it tolls for thee." When we discover this, we master the second dimension of life.

Finally, there is a third dimension. Some people never get beyond the first two dimensions of life. They master the first two. They develop their inner powers; they love humanity; but they stop right here. They end up with the feeling that man is the end of all things and that humanity is God. Philosophically or theologically, many of them would call themselves humanists. They seek to live life without a sky. They find themselves bogged down on the horizontal plane without being integrated on the vertical plane. But if we are to live the complete life we must reach up and discover God. H. G. Wells was right: "The man who is not religious begins at nowhere and ends at nothing." Religion is like a mighty wind that breaks down doors and makes that possible and even easy which seems difficult and impossible.

In our modern world it is easy for us to forget this. We so often find ourselves unconsciously neglecting this third dimension of life. Not that we go up and say, "Good-by, God, we are going to leave you now." But we become so involved in the things of this world that we are unconsciously carried away by the rushing tide of materialism which leaves us treading in the confused waters of secularism. We find ourselves living in what Professor Sorokin of Harvard called a sensate civilization, believing that only those things which we can see and touch and to which we can apply our five senses have existence.

Something should remind us once more that the great things in this universe are things that we never see. You walk out at night and look up at the beautiful stars as they bedeck the heavens like swinging lanterns of eternity, and you think you can see all. Oh, no. You can never see the law of gravitation that holds them there. You walk around this vast campus and you probably have a great esthetic experience as I have had walking about and looking at the beautiful buildings, and you think you see all. Oh, no. You can never see the mind of the architect who drew the blueprint. You can never see the love and the faith and the hope of the individuals who made it so. You look at me and you think you see Martin Luther King. You don't see Martin Luther King; you see my body, but, you must understand, my body can't think, my body can't reason. You don't see the me that makes me me. You can never see my personality.

In a real sense everything that we see is a shadow cast by that which we do not see. Plato was right: "The visible is a shadow cast by the invisible." And so God is still around. All of our new knowledge, all of our new developments, cannot diminish his being one iota. These new advances have banished God neither from the microcosmic compass of the atom nor from the vast, unfathomable ranges of interstellar space. The more we learn about this universe, the more mysterious and awesome it becomes. God is still here.

So I say to you, seek God and discover him and make him a power in your life. Without him all of our efforts turn to ashes and our sunrises into darkest nights. Without him, life is a meaningless drama with the decisive scenes missing. But with him we are able to rise from the fatigue of despair to the buoyancy of hope. With him we are able to rise from the midnight of desperation to the daybreak of joy. Saint Augustine was right—we were made for God and we will be restless until we find rest in him.

Love yourself, if that means rational, healthy, and moral self-interest. You are commanded to do that. That is the length of life. Love your neighbor as you love yourself. You are commanded to do that. That is the breadth of life. But never forget that there is a first and even greater commandment, "Love the Lord thy God with all thy heart and all thy soul and all thy mind." This is the height of life. And when you do this you live the complete life.

Thank God for John who, centuries ago, caught a vision of the new Jerusalem. God grant that those of us who still walk the road of life will catch this vision and decide to move forward to that city of complete life in which the length and the breadth and the height are equal.

O God, our gracious heavenly Father, we thank thee for all of the insights of the ages, and we thank thee for the privilege of having fellowship with thee. Help us to discover ourselves, to discover our neighbors, and to discover thee, and to make all part of our life. Grant that we will go now with grim and bold determination to live the complete life. In the name and spirit of Jesus, we pray. Amen.

Parting

We've got some difficult days ahead. But it really doesn't matter with me now. Because I've been to the mountaintop. I won't mind. Like anybody, I would like to live a long life. Longevity has its place. But I'm not concerned about that now. I just want to do God's will.

And he's allowed me to go up to the mountain. And I've looked over, and I've seen the Promised Land. I may not get there with you, but I want you to know tonight that we as a people will get to the Promised Land.

So I'm happy tonight. I'm not worried about anything. I'm not fearing any man. "Mine eyes have seen the glory of the coming of the Lord."

Martin Luther King Jr.
April 3, 1968